MORTAL RECOLLECTIONS

A JOURNEY THROUGH THE VARIOUS ASPECTS OF LIFE AND THE COUNTLESS UNEXPLAINED EMOTIONS.

MOKSHI AGGARWAL

*I HUMBLY AND MOST RESPECTFULLY
DEDICATE THIS BOOK TO MY ENGLISH
TEACHER MR. GAURAV, WHO
ENLIGHTENED ME WITH NUMEROUS
LIFE LESSONS AND ENCOURAGED ME
TO KEEP WRITING.*

Contents

Contents

MORTAL RECOLLECTIONS

Preface

Being a teenager, I realised there are so many things in life that cannot be elucidated. The beauty of the Universe is in it's bewildering nature.In this labyrinth, we face so many crossroads where differentiating between right and wrong becomes challenging.Interpretation of the easiest of emotions becomes an obstacle.No doubt, we don't know how to face these issues but when we find examples of people facing the same dillemas we get a ray of hope that maybe it's okay, and it's not a big deal not to know the answer to all the questions life poses at us. So, this anthology recounts a mortal's sundry beliefs and interactions experienced throughout life in poetic form. These inexplicable things cannot be decoded but we all can relate to them. Hope you find all your feelings in this Pandora Box.

RAIN

RAIN, A BRIDGE THAT CONNECTS SOULS

Rain comes,
on my soft little hands
with a mug of hot chocolate
and endless flashbacks
flashbacks of you, me and us
memories of joys and laughter.

Rain soaks me...
I recall your affectionate smiles
I forget my dreadful sorrows
and there comes the rainbow
a reunion so sweet and complete to my heart.
Oh brother! If only you were here.

BEACH

*THE TRANSCENDENTAL HAPPINESS OF
SERENITY.*

*The sunny day at the beach,
the golden sand in my reach,
makes my heart pure as gold;
flowing into the ocean's rhythm,
like water into a mold.*

*It's the sound of the sea
it's the silence of that sound
the emerald waters
reminding me of the endless joys*

Leaving the world behind,
I feel each wave
giving me just a caress
to relieve me of the day.

LAVENDERS

LAVENDER IS ABSTRACTLY PURE LOVE.

*The lavenders drifting blissfully
in the purple field
with merry laughs
and serene smiles*

*That scent so mesmerizing
I lose my sense of time
humming tunes,
reminding me of each moment
I cherish with my heart.*

*The lilac hue
still enchants me,*

I lose this world
to love my own echo.
the best thing
that ever happened to me
is coming to this Lavender meadow.

SECOND CHANCE

THERE ARE NO SECOND CHANCES, SO
IF GOD GIVES YOU ONE, CHERISH IT.

Ruffling leaves
Baffling heights
Shuffling sheets
Your lies so white.

Quit saying 'I love it'
if you lived your aim,
you would've studied
if you lived your goal,
by stress, you wouldn't have been buried
start saying 'I embrace you'
and work hard.
once again,
Start...

WONDERLAND

WONDERAND- AN ESCAPE FROM THE REAL WORLD, BUT DON'T LET IT RUIN THE REAL YOU.

I'm never hungry
I'm just sleepy
escaping the real world
to my sweety
I have no choice,
I have to abandon it
I have no voice
I have to conceal it

Don't let your anxiety outsmart you
don't let your fears weaken you
don't let any wonderland,
get a hold of you.

SWEAT & BLOOD

MY LIFE, MY STRUGGLE, MY JOY.

Sweat and blood are precious
spend them on something delicious
don't waste all your efforts
in hiding the truth
don't waste your breath
in telling lies
it's a vast world
it's a small life

Live it so you love it
cherish every moment
as an experience for the unknown
the exhilaration of what lies ahead
is the real thrill,
so, never back out.

LIVE ON

WE HAVE TO KEEP LIVING, ENDING
LIVES IS NOT AN OPTION.

We spend our lives
trying to find dreams,
we live our lives
fulfilling our dreams,
we enjoy our lives
sharing our dreams,
we end our lives
shattering our dreams,

Why not live on and
give life a second chance
Like it gave you countless times?
Why always be so rigid
And end up ending everything

TITANIC

ALL IT EVER TAKES IS COURAGE

Titanic and Robert were two big ships
Titanic was brave and ready to fight the waves
Robert was a cowardly ship
Titanic died in the storms
but it's still alive in our hearts
Robert was too scared to swim in the sea,
that it rusted in the harbour, yet not in glee
none of the two is there now
Yet, we remember Titanic but Robert is unknown
Because Titanic took the plunge and Robert did not.

THE QUEEN

A FIGHT AGAINST OPPRESSION, INJUSTICE, INEQUALITY AND THE MONARCH.

Blue is the sky
with gloom and sadness,
Red is my rage
for you your highness,
Yellow is the field
of corns all ripened,
I'll never yield,
it's a promise I'll harness.

White are your lies,
black is your heart;
go away your highness
before I tear you apart.

THANK YOU

REMEMBER TO REMEMBER ALL
THOSE WONDERFUL PEOPLE WHO
MAKE YOUR LIFE BEAUTIFUL.

Thank you mom, for staying up with me those countless nights
Thank you dad, for saving me from mom's beatings countless times

Thank you friend for encouraging me each time I fell
Thank you brother, for loving me all the times alone I felt.

Thank you sister, for finding every excuse to give me presents.
Thank you ma'am, for putting in effort and giving me life's essence.

Thank you love, for showing me the magical healing power of affection.
You all make me better bit by bit, I am your support's reflection.

TRAITOR

NOT ALL DEVILS WEAR BLACK CAPES,
SOME WEAR BEAUTIFUL SMILES.

That facade of trust
I'm still comprehending,
that pain of hurt
is never ending,
your choice of word
is quite offending,
you left me up above
all alone... still defending

VENUS

Dusk till dawn
you are with me
making me feel free
making everything alright
but let the evening star bright
kiss the world tonight
you lost me love,
somewhere...
in this space
or above,
leaving me in despair,
lonely as a dove.

CATALYST

ANY FRIEND, GUIDE OR MENTOR CAN BE YOUR CATALYST, AS LONG THERE IS MUTUAL TRUST.

You are my sunshine
you are my pain
looking at you shining bright
vanishes all my pain

They say it's fantasy,
so what if it is.
You prompt me to improve,
you are my catalyst.

SOULMATE

NOT ALL SOULMATES ARE LOVERS.

I met that person for the very first time
I saw something enigmatic and so divine,
I felt that connection across millennia,
Telling me this person was someone very special
A pleading from my soul,
Seeking that person's presence
A soulmate who was meant to drift.

TALISMAN

MY FINEST ARMOUR, MY DAD.

You have all the magical powers
You are my good luck
Your charms fix everything,
My genie, you fulfill all my wishes.
The only who who can revamp me.
Warding off all my evil,
You are my talisman,
You are my lovely dad.

RETRIBUTION

ONE CAN NEVER ESCAPE THE CHAINS OF RETRIBUTION.

You left me, somewhere...
somewhere like a fish out of water,
like the broken wand of Harry Potter,
like beans for a mortar,
like mud for an otter,

Somewhere...
deep in the ocean;
it's my retribution,
tells me my intuition.

NOSTALGIA

BRAVERY & COURAGE ARE NOT ALWAYS GLORIFIED, SOMETIMES, THEY ARE JUST LEFT... RUSTING.

The rust on these hinges
Recite an untold lore,
of courage and bravery.
But will justice uphold
for those windows of gold
which once let in light
as the Sun showed its golden face
and the sunshine poured?

Will we get back what we lost?
Will innocence fade away
As intelligence comes close?

Let us join hands to thank our younger selves
For the countless times it saved us, taught us
And made us who we are today.

SMILE AND KEEP MOVING

A POSITIVE OUTLOOK GIVES POSITIVE RESULTS.

The life of a person
too long to panic
too short to regret
too hard to go soft
too precious to let go
too dear to give up

So just smile and keep moving
learn and keep growing
because it's always snowing
for some to make snowman
for some to get stuck in houses
what about you?

FACE THE TRUTH

Let us all gather
to belittle and flatter
the promises that scatter

Can't find my ailment but I've got the cure
the promises contaminated
have made me pure.

MIGHT

*YOU GOT COURAGE? NOTHING CAN
STOP YOU.*

*Walking alone
On the dusty road
With willows so long,
I can't see my abode.*

*There is eternal hope,
There is a bright life
Where there is might.*

ROLLER COASTER

Ups and downs, slow or fast,
fascinating yet scary
screams of joy and
cries of fear

You think you'll fall
but remember you've got the belt
so, as long as you trust
you can make it happen

Riding the roller coaster
of life is inevitable,
but laughs or cries,
the option is yours.

KARMA

***THE ONLY PERPETUAL MOTION
MACHINE THAT PRACTICALLY WORKS.***

*For me, it's a dream
For you, it may be a nightmare
You don't trust karma
Cause you yourself lie
I embrace karma
Because I was always honest.*

*I believe heaven sees everything
You'll get what you deserve
And I'll get mine.
No matter how hard you try
You can't run away from your reality,
Doesn't matter who you are.
Remember... Always...
Karma puts you in your place.*

LOST

LOST... SOMEWHERE, SOMEWHEN, IN YOU

There at the seaside
I sit with my notebook
my world of fantasy
a work of dreams

Dreaming something about someone
who used to be me
I write to myself
but forget when it becomes
all about you...

And I'm all immersed in thoughts
not realising my champagne glass
fleeting away into waves
leaving me behind in caves
my pen moves to write my thoughts
not realising, I write your name

EL- DORADO

SOMETIMES FAITH WORKS WHERE
SCIENCE DOESN'T.

The fabled city of gold,
the fabled world of love
none t'is true
yet I die for you.
in your eyes shining bright, let me lie
at your smile perfectly right, let me die

No city found,
no gold discovered
yet I live there for my lover,
longing, for a miracle to occur.

LAST GLANCE

AS WE ENTER NEW DOORS, WE HAVE
TO LEAVE THE OLDER ONES AS IT IS,
BUT... IS IT REALLY THAT EASY?

I keep saying 'this chapter is over'
Yet I come back over and over
I remind myself
I have to move on
But forget when you put your smile on.

One day, I'll forget you
I'll not care 'bout you
I have dreams to achieve
I have hope to believe
That I will succeed
So, I must give myself a chance
To work for my real self, but a last glance.

KNIGHT

*YOU SAVE LIVES BUT WHY DIDN'T YOU
SAVE ME WHEN I FELL (FOR YOU)?*

*All gloom goes away at his sight
Oh! my dear knight.
tears in his eyes,
like pearls so bright.*

*Admiring him is my right
but loving him requires might.
though he stands at great height,
I hope he can see my light
that shines for him every night
as the thought of leaving him,
gives me fright.*

LAZY MAN

THIS LABYRINTH LIKE SOCIETY IS NOT FOR US INDOLENTS.

Strange world
stranger still, it's people
one bad, omnipresent feeling
making me forget all my responsibilities
making me worthless
laziness, well... it's mine

PERIODIC TABLE

FOR SOME, EDUCATON IS NOT JUST TRANSFER OF KNOWLEDGE, IT'S A SPIRITUAL BELIEF.

My dearie, my only partner,my periodic table
like a mantra,
you enchant me with your beauty

from (H) hydrogen to (Og) Oganneson,
You are always there.

Reciting your love songs,
Calms me down eternally
My guide,
through the toughest times,
my periodic table.